AS THE FIRES CONTINUE TO BURN

As The Fires Continue To Burn

by
Carlo Crozatti

American Literary Press

Owings Mills, Maryland

As The Fires Continue To Burn

Copyright © 1992 Carlo Crozatti

All rights reserved under International and Pan-American copyright conventions. No part of this book may be reproduced, stored in a retrieval system or transmitted in any form, electronic, mechanical, or other means, now known or hereafter invented, without written permission of the author. Address all inquiries to the author.

Library of Congress
Cataloging in Publication Data
ISBN 1-56167-096-0

Published by

American Literary Press
11419 Cronridge Drive #10
Owings Mills, Maryland 21117

Manufactured in the United States of America

DEDICATION:

To Mama & Papa

For supplying the proper

poetic atmosphere

in every place

we ever called

our home

MEMBER OF:

Georgia Freelance Writers Association

Phoenix Writer's Service

Manuscript Market Technologies, Inc.

INDEX

Page . . .

11. Introduction

12. The Final Curtain

14. The Best Man?

16. Hail To Queen Renee'

18. Ode To Man's Best Friend

21. My Last Hunt

23. Anamnesis

25. Lunation

27. A Rainy Day

29. The Lady Who Made Me Dance

31. Prelude To Death Of Jennifer

33. Requiem For A Fickle Lady

35. My Lone Irish Rose

37. The Political Trees
(From Judges 9:8)

INDEX
(Continued)

39. Ode To A Hummingbird

40. I Forgot To Forget

42. Lora

44. Our Last Night

46. Rhapsodiac

48. London Bridge

50. To A Weeping Willow

52. A Una Cantatrice Speciale
(Albergo Americano di Roma)

54. View From Sissy's Window

56. To An Anonymous Lover

58. Jones Lake

60. Invidia

62. Humoresque In Rhyme

67. Man In The Moon Over Douglas

68. Eyes On The Sparrow

70. Ode To My Sister Ruby

72. . Charlie, Gladys, And Me

INDEX
(Continued)

74. Hold The Baby

76. To A Roman Tree

78. Western Sky Watch

79. Family Affair

80. Lake Watch

81. Weather Forecast

82. If I Failed To Love You

85. Merry Christmas, Ltd.

87. Guest Poets Section

INTRODUCTION

This is my third volume of published poetry. The first was titled, "All Of My Best To You," the second was called, "As The Fires Burned."

Being that this third volume contains many pieces complimentary, or, perhaps, even symbiotic to some found in the last two volumes, it was decided that it should be called, "As The Fires Continue To Burn'

It is a foregone conclusion, accepted by most of my regular readers -- one of whom I hope you will soon become -- my entire repertoire can be capsulated in just three words, "I Love You!"

You see, dear one, when a poet says, "I love you," it is not a banal expression; it comes not from the lips nor from the heart alone...

When a poet says I love you, it is a trilogy orchestrated by Erato, and performed by the lips, the heart and the soul of the poet.

When a poet says, "I love you," it reverberates through boundless ages of eternity to be sanctioned by bards past, present, and future. The coda being, "So mote it be!"

And so, irregardless of the fact we may never have met in the flesh, the very fact that you are reading this prelude confirms that certain affinity which exists only between poets and lovers. Ergo, I loved you even As The Fires Continue To Burn.

CARLO CROZATTI

12 - As The Fires Continue To Burn

THE FINAL CURTAIN*

It's over!
Our little charade has ended.
It's over!
But not in the way we intended.
The drama we planned was so clever,
But we both knew right from the start
That the play wouldn't run forever;
But what do I tell my poor heart?

It's over!
The bravos have died in the air.
It's over!
The end of a thespian affair.
We've made our last bow together,
And smiled through our final encore.
Only heaven above knows whether
We'll answer the call anymore.

It's over!
Except for the final good-bye.

My Best To You

It's over!

The script doesn't say we can't cry . . .

You played your part like a pro, dear,

And now the curtain must fall;

But how were we to know, dear,

That our hearts were not acting at all?

It's over!

So I'd better be on my way.

It's over!

The marquee reads, "Closing today."

Tell your next leading man when you find him,

Never to leave you alone;

For I'll be standing behind him,

And, darling, the show must go on.

1988 WOP $1000 Golden Poet Award

14 - As The Fires Continue To Burn

THE BEST MAN?

This letter I write to you, sweetheart,
(Though I will never send it),
Confessing my world is torn apart,
And now there's none to mend it.

I act'd as best man at your wedding,
And all the rules I kept--
I fought the tears my eyes were shedding,
But in my heart I wept.

Oh, how my arms ached to enfold you--
And how my soul did cry . . .
So many things I should have told you,
But let my chance go by.

I love you, love, what more to say--
Except I thought you knew?
How could you not have seen the way
My heart reached out to you?

My Best To You

I wanted you to know the way
I've always felt about you--
Now only God alone can say
If I can live without you.

So I'll just close as I began,
A poor, sad, wretched mome--
You see, I was the NEXT best man,
The BEST man took you home.

16 - As The Fires Continue To Burn

HAIL TO QUEEN RENEE

SHE APPEARS

and I see

Waterfalls of burnished gold

cascading over pillars of Italian marble

SHE GLANCES

and I see

two precious gems

sparkling their appreciation to the gods

for having endowed them with colours

unique and foreign

to all other gems

SHE SMILES

and I see

the birth of a lotus blossom

born from the kiss of a pomegranate

My Best To You

SHE SPEAKS

and Euterpe sighs

as his orchestra

from sheer admiration

forbears to play their instruments of mirth

SHE IS

the Queen

Long live the Queen!

Viva Queen Renee!

18 - As The Fires Continue To Burn

TO MAN'S BEST FRIEND

Among my fondest memories
Of when I was a lad,
Is my first and dearest friend--
An old dog I once had.

Oh, no! he wasn't exceptional,
Didn't know a single trick;
But of love and loyalty,
You just couldn't beat ol' Nick.

We'd roam the fields in search of game,
Most of the times in vain;
But I knew Nick was doing his best,
So how could I complain?

The thing that always puzzled me,
That seemed almost a sin,
Was, though Nick had the longest legs,
The game would always win.

My Best To You

Ol' Nick would lose on hills, in swamps,
In sunshine or in rain;
But, as I look back on the years,
I think I can explain.

You see, just like the man who runs
Life's race for goods that's rife,
Ol' Nick was running a meal-
The game was running for his life.

Then came the day to say "good-bye"
To my old faithful hound.
You see, some "hunters" far away
Would claim our hunting ground.

Now, as I look back on that day,
It seems somehow he knew
That our next hunt would be the fields
Of lands beyond the blue.

When I came home to see ol' Nick
'fore heading over seas,
He licked my hand then turned away
And vanished among the trees.

20 - As The Fires Continue To Burn

I made it back home from the war
To find 'ol Nick had gone
To join the big hunt in the sky,
And I was left alone.

Sometimes when I see shapely clouds
Race 'cross the sky so free,
I wonder if my old friend, Nick
Is searching clouds for me.

Well, anyway, it won't be long
Before ol' Nick and I
Will be together once again,
To roam that endless sky.

So, fare well, old faithful hound,
Many happy trails to you;
And tell Orion to make room,
For I'll soon be there too.

My Best To You

MY LAST HUNT

I walked alone

away from Papa

I came upon

a small, chilled bunny

sitting snugly against a stump

It did not run away

I wondered why

I glanced at the gun in my hand

I think the bunny saw it too

but it was not afraid

As those soft brown eyes stared at me

my mind unfurled

back to that giddy day

in the pet shop in Capo Di Chino

when you said to me

22 - As The Fires Continue To Burn

"My next trip to this planet

will be as a little brown bunny"

When I asked why?

You said

"Because you love bunnies so much"

I smiled

and

the bunny twitched its nose

exactly the way you used to

The wind was cold

My eyes watered terribly

I removed the shells from my gun

waved good-bye to bunny

and

without calling to papa

walked back across the field

home

never to go rabbit hunting

again

My Best To You

ANAMNESIS*

From the balcony of my hotel room
I watched the grand parade.
The yellow bows,
The "ahs" and "ohs,"
The clamour the revellers made.

My mind unfurled to other times--
I fought to squelch a sob--
They said, "Not war,
We need you for
A short policing job".

It was a scene in which our guys
All played the "fall guy" role.
Months turned to years,
Smiles turned to tears--
For some the bells yet toll.

Finally the long awaited trek
Back to the homes we'd left.
To find no "Thanks!"
No "Welcome, Yanks!"
Of honour, we were bereft.

24 - As The Fires Continue To Burn

No "Welcome home," with grand parades--
No bands, no flags, no bows . . .
No ribbons tied,
No show of pride,
No billboards for heroes.

They treated us as violent rogues
Who, of our own accord,
Left mills and farms
To take up arms
And launched mayhem abroad."

No one took time to realize
That doughboys had no say:-
Where they were sent--
What orders meant--
Our lot was to obey.

If only memories could die
As brave as soldiers do;
We'd all forget
The term "Viet"
And pledge our cause anew.

1991 WOP $1000 Golden Poet Award

My Best To You

LUNATION

Another moon has waned, my love,
Since last I saw your face;
And felt the touch
I love so much,
Which no one can replace.

At dusk today I saw a star;
It winked as though it knew
That you are gone
And I'm alone,
And both our worlds are blue.

This eve I muse on simple things:
Red sunsets, parks, and lanes;
Long grassy hills,
And sweet jonquils--
Long strolls after the rains.

Zephyrus blows his breath across
The garden where we met--
The perfumes rise
To smart the eyes...
Alas, my cheeks are wet.

As The Fires Burn

26 - As The Fires Continue To Burn

Tonight, sweetheart, I said a prayer
To Him who's our retreat--
That He'll be near
To you, my dear,
And make our love complete.

Before another moon shall wane,
May all the gods agree--
Whether hills or home,
Where'er I roam,
There shall you also be.

A RAINY DAY

O sad and dreary, rainy day,
Why bring your showers of gloom?
You hide the sun
From everyone--
For joy there is no room.

You line the walks with muddy pools
That we will have to wade;
Small tots at play
Must run away
Until your showers fade.

The little elves must run and find
A haven from your showers--
They mustn't get
Their nimbi wet,
Or they'd lose all their powers.

O sad and dreary, rainy day,
Please go, I beg of you!
Your work is done,
You've spoiled our fun--
Now bid the world adieu.

28 - As The Fires Continue To Burn

Good-bye, O sad and rainy day,

So long little drops of rain--

Just disappear,

The sky is clear;

The sun is out again.

THE LADY WHO MADE ME DANCE

It was the Poets' Mardi Gras,
And from around the world,
Scores of bards let down their hair,
And laughed, and spun, and whirled.

The band was playing New Orleans jazz
With down home bluesy beats--
And even the staid sophisticates
Were swaying in their seats.

I sat and watched the different moods,
From frivolous to romance--
Then smiled when I remembered that
I never did learn to dance.

Then she stepped up and took my hand,
And led me down the aisle--
Oblivious of my vain protest
That dancing weren't my style.

30 - As The Fires Continue To Burn

To my surprise, I made a pas-
Then two, and three, and four.
Then, led by her mesmeric charms,
We danced around the floor.

We started with a simple step,
But 'fore the night was over;
She had me doing a classic thing
She called "The Bossa Nova."

The memory of that magic night
Shall long live in my heart--
Her mental choreography
Was sheer poetic art.

Now when I hear those jazzy beats,
With pomp and circumstance;
My mind goes back to New Orleans,
And the Lady who made me dance.

My Best To You

PRELUDE TO THE DEATH OF JENNIFER

She wasn't beautiful

she wasn't smart

but

she was mine

mine until

that terrible day of perdition

when she confessed to me

that

she was in love

with

another man

that was the day

I shook hands with death

then

after days

32 - As The Fires Continue To Burn

weeks and months

of

unsuccessful toil

trying to purge her from my mind

I concluded that

Jennifer's death was the only antidote

for my inevitable insanity

yes

Jennifer had to die

I searched for days

but

my only weapon was

my trusty old typewriter

ergo

Requiem For A Fickle Lady!

My Best To You

REQUIEM FOR A FICKLE LADY*

Many springs have come and gone
Since you were called away --
I miss the sound
Of you around
To brighten up my day.

They said the hurt would go away
On wings of the "Silver Dove."
How wrong they were,
My Jennifer,
You're still my only love.

We both knew you were never true,
But lies can be so sweet . . .
That taunting smile,
While all the while,
A new love you would meet.

So many times we walked away
And said we'd call it quits,
Only to find
That in our mind
We both were hypocrites.

As The Fires Burn

34 - As The Fires Continue To Burn

Although I was apprised of your
Capricious life and style,
My soul would yearn
For your return
To hold me for awhile.

My heart tells me that even now
Your paramours are rife . . .
Can someone there
Possibly care
As I did in this life?

Oh, Jennifer, my heart, my soul!
Why did you have to leave?
My heart yet cries,
And slowly dies . . .
My soul weeps for reprieve.

Although, I'm reconciled to live
With memories impearled--
When this life's through,
I'll search for you
In yet another world.

1990 APA $1000 Poet Of Merit Award

My Best To You

MY LONE IRISH ROSE

The great symposium had come to an end,
The poets were just milling around;
When out of the masses,
Stepped two lovely lassies
Who started my old heart to pound.

They greeted me gently and gave me a hug,
Sending chills from my head to my toes...
"We love your life style,"
They said with a smile;
Then gave me one lone Irish rose.

I fought back the tears that welled in my eyes,
For strangers must ne'er see me cry;
But down in my heart,
I knew from the start
Those tears would burst free by and by.

I whispered my thanks as I kissed both their hands
With feelings that God only knows.
To think that they cared
Enough that they shared
With me by way of a rose.

36 - As The Fires Continue To Burn

Of all the awards I've ever received
(All rightly deserved, I suppose);
But, lone on a shelf,
In a place by itself,
Lies my beautiful lone Irish rose.

"God bless ISP," will my prayer ever be,
For a sonnet that'll lie in repose . . .
It'll share a blest part
In the trove of my heart
With two lassies and m'lone Irish rose.

My Best To You

THE POLITICAL TREES

(From Judges 9:8)

The trees went forth to find a king
To rule their forest domain--
They went from giant oak to sapling
To find one who would reign.

They searched the woods and came across
The wise old Olive Tree--
He shook his limbs, displayed his floss,
Then said with dignity:

"Should I consent to play the fool
And alter nature's plan,
Wherewith my fatness, as a rule,
Honours both God and man?"

Oh no! I can't betray my God
In search of worldly fame--
To change my state would be a fraud.
I will not play your game.

38 - As The Fires Continue To Burn

They asked the Fig Tree if he would
Consider their royal coup--
He said, "I'll ask God if I should,
And what He says, I'll do.

Then, as they watched the wise old fig,
He grimaced and then he frowned--
"There's no percentage in playing big,
Thanks, but I'll stand my ground."

They searched and searched only to find
That trees valued God's trust--
The thought was tempting to the mind,
But none succumbed to lust.

Just like the trees we sometime face
The Tempter's nth degrees--
But, thanks to God's amazing grace,
We're even more wise than trees.
P. S. Or, are we?

My Best To You

ODE TO A HUMMINGBIRD

Hello, little thirsty hummingbird,
Now don't you be afraid--
You have a yen for sweets, I've heard,
Come, share my lemonade.

You flap your little wings so fast,
And flit from place to place--
Your beauty, I'll bet, is unsurpassed,
Come, let me see your face.

Fly in a wee bit closer now,
Bring in your wings and land--
Come take a sip, I'll show you how;
Here, come sit in my hand.

Don't leave, my little humming friend,
Come back! don't fly away!...
(I guess he just didn't comprehend,
For he just flew away.)

40 - As The Fires Continue To Burn

I FORGOT TO FORGET

I forgot to forget to remember
The thrill of your hand touching mine--
Our walks in summer rain,
Your smile through pink champagne,
And lips that are sweeter than wine.

I forgot to forget to remember
I still have your ring and your glove.
With all my soul I'm trying,
But my heart just isn't buying . . .
I forgot to forget I'm in love.

I forgot to forget to remember
That dreams are so hard to command--
And, tho we're worlds apart,
You're always in my heart--
Darling, my life is in your hand.

I forgot to forget to remember
My heart beats no longer for you.
Your lips say you don't want me,
But memories still haunt me . . .
I forgot to forget to be blue.

My Best To You

Poetry By Carlo Crozatti - 41

I forgot to forget to remember

The promise we made when we met . . .

Let's listen to our heart,

And go back to the start--

Let's forget to remember to forget.

LORA

Lora,
With the hair of flame,
And lips like Roman wine;
Her eyes would put the stars to shame,
Sparkling with love divine.

Lora,
With the kiss of fire
That brands the souls of men,
And turns each thought into desire
For prizes they can't win.

Lora,
With the smiling face,
She smiles and light breaks through.
Her voice is like a sweet embrace,
Her touch's a burning coal.

Lora,
With euphonic laugh
That flows like tropic streams--
Like some long-treasured photograph
That haunts a lover's dream.

My Best To You

Lora,

With the hair of flame,

And eyes Romana blue;

Be still, my heart, she's just a game--

She'll never belong to you.

44 - As The Fires Continue To Burn

OUR LAST NIGHT IN CASERIA

Last night

as you would take your leave of me

you reached out

and

oh so gently touched my arm

Then

you pressed your face against my chest

and my soul cried

cried because

my arms were unable

to fulfill the command

from my heart

You see my love

my heart commanded

that my arms reach out to you

My Best To You

and to

gather all of you

unto

all of me

but

that night had a hundred eyes

eyes which could have

misinterpreted

my amorous reciprocity of your

platonic tenderness

and so tonight

my love

my heart cries

cries because

of

our last night

As The Fires Burn

46 - As The Fires Continue To Burn

RHAPSODIAC

I stroll across the dewy lea,
Acknowledged by the chicadee;
Fain that the woods remember me--
Trying to forget Olga.

I watch the leaves dance in the breeze
As autumn winds caress the trees
With melancholic rhapsodies--
And I remember Olga.

I stare into the sinking sun
As day and night transmute to one,
And wonder, briefly, which is done--
Reminding me of Olga.

I watch the twilight as it wane,
And shadows steal across the plain--
A tear my soul could not contain
Displays my thoughts of Olga.

My Best To You

I watch whitetail descend the trail,

And hear the lonely nightingale

Extol his amouristic wail;

And I, then, weep for Olga.

As The Fires Burn

48 - As The Fires Continue To Burn

LONDON BRIDGE

There is a ditty in a book,
Its words for granted I'm 'fraid I took:
It says somewhere in London Town
A certain bridge is falling down.

I saw it once-today, in fact-
A little worn, but yet intact.
I gave a shove to make real sure
Its ancient limbs were quite secure.

I'm not quite sure, and I shan't lie,
But it seemed to heave a sigh . . .
As if to say, "Aye, there you see
That song of woe was not of me.

"For I am here, still strong and tall;
And, sir, I'm not about to fall.
Forsooth, I'm old, but doff your fears;
For strength and wisdom come with years.

My Best To You

Poetry By Carlo Crozatti - 49

"Though trials assailed in every form,
By Jove, I've weathered every storm.
So, please convey to all you meet
That London Bridge defies defeat!"

And so, with due respect to all,
My former thoughts I must recall:
For I am well convinced today
That London Bridge is here to stay.

TO A WEEPING WILLOW

O lovely Willow on the hill,
Surrounded by the sweet jonquil--
Why do you weep this early morn?
Can a willow be lovelorn?

Was there a sapling of your own,
And now you weep because she's gone?
Rememb'ring sharing sun and rain
And now never to touch again.

O Willow with a thousand eyes!
With you this bard does empathize;
For I, like you, were once a pair,
Linked to a maiden young and fair.

And, like your sapling, so my maid,
Was lured into another glade--
And I, like you, was left in tears
To face the lonely, loveless years.

O weeping Willow, let's be friends,
Comrades together until time ends!
A weeping willow--a lonely boy--
From hence our tears will be of joy.

So weep, my friend, now that we know
The meaning of each tear that flow;
This hill will be our rendezvous--
You weep for me and I for you.

O lovely Willow on the hill,
Surrounded by the sweet jonquil--
Why do you weep this early morn?
"I weep for joy, for I'm reborn!"

52 - As The Fires Continue To Burn

A UNA CANTATRICE SPECIALE

(Albergo Americano di Roma)

Who will you sing to tonight, cara mia,
Such themes as pyramids along the Nile?
Will you sing to him of things
Like missions bells and rings?
Will you sing about the lady's mystic smile?

Will you sing to him of Gypsy caravans?
Of ladies who can drive away your fear?
Should he kiss you tenderly,
Will the vow you made to me,
Like the smoke from cigarettes, just disappear?

Will you sit by his chair on the carpet
And sing of magic places far away?
Will he know that you're not free --
That your heart belongs to me --
That this is just a game torch singers play?

When his fingers softly touch your lips so tender--

The fire of Eros burning with delight;

In this moment meant for two,

When his arms reach out to you,

Will my love help you to make it through the night?

Who will you sing to tonight, cara mia?

Oh, how my wretched heart the gods implore!

May Euterpe lose his charms

Till you're back within my arms--

Then let His music play for evermore.

As The Fires Burn

54 - As The Fires Continue To Burn

VIEW FROM SISSY'S WINDOW

I watch the sun slip down behind
The dogwoods in the west--
A playful breeze
rustles the trees,
Then settles down to rest.

Orion now makes his entree gran,
Artemis ascends the sea--
Aeolus begins
His violins
Of dogwood symphony.

Sounds that surround me by the day
Are silenced by the night--
Across the vale,
Sir nightingale
Crows his nocturnal right.

I watch a lonely deer limp by
Draped in the waning light--
Then from the brush,
A mother thrush,
Is settling for the night.

My Best To You

Out of the darkness, I can hear
Medleys of nighttime prate--
A turtle dove,
Enrapt with love,
Is cooing for his mate.

The sun has quietly slipped away--
Darkness subdues the light--
Ergo, to you,
I bid adieu,
And fade into the night.

56 - As The Fires Continue To Burn

TO AN ANONYMOUS LOVER

Another moon has waned, my love,
Since last I saw your face;
And felt the touch
I love so much,
Which no one can replace.

At dusk today I saw a star,
It winked as though it knew
That you are gone
And I'm alone;
And both our worlds are blue.

This eve I muse on simple things,
Red sunsets, parks, and lanes;
Long grassy hills
And sweet jonquils--
Long strolls after the rains.

Zephyrus blows his breath across
The garden where we met--
The perfumes rise
To smart the eyes. Alas, my cheeks are wet.
Tonight, sweetheart, I said a prayer

My Best To You

To Him who's our retreat--
That He'll be near
To you, my dear,
And make our love complete.

Before another moon shall wane,
May all the gods agree--
Whether hills or home,
Where'er I roam,
There shall you also be.

As The Fires Burn

58 - As The Fires Continue To Burn

JONES LAKE

Upon the west bank of Jones Lake,
'Neath an Australian pine,
I stare with grief
And disbelief
On environs decline.

Where once there flowed a crystal lake
Far as the eye could see,
Is now become
A grim sanctum
For man's toxic debris.

Bottles, beer cans, and plastic cups,
Where carp and trout once ran--
A monument
Of malcontent,
And carelessness of man.

Gone are the fields of chinquapin
Where coneys used to hide--
When Chippewa
And hyena
Both hunted side by side.

My Best To You

Poetry By Carlo Crozatti

The golden days when little papoose
"Speared killifish" in the sand--
As brave Mwindo
And Min ne-ho
Strolled day watch hand in hand.

No more the windsong can we sing,
Unwanted tones appear . . .
Of slaughtered trees,
Giant factories
Fauna of yesteryear.

No more the smell of parching maze
Beckons Hiawatha home
To bison steak,
And pepon cake--
Chufas and honeycomb.

So, as the tall, dark shadows fall,
Hiding my tears from sight--
I, like the day,
Just fade away...
Thankful for shades of night.

As The Fires Burn

60 - As The Fires Continue To Burn

INVIDIA

What lies behind yon mount of flame
Where Sol doth now descend?
Perhaps a world of fantasia
Where cares and worries end.

Perhaps elusive Shangri-la
Behind that mount is lain--
The gateway to idyllic bliss,
Where joy and pleasure reign.

Oh, if I but had the power
To travel as the sun,
I'd lave the world with rays of hope
And peace for everyone.

I'd search the world for hearts that broke
From dreams that ne'er came true;
Then I would summon all my charms
And mend them all anew.

My Best To You

There'd be no time for cares and woes,

And wars would be unknown.

I'd be a friend to everyone--

No man would be alone.

Alas, but I am but a man

Trapped in life's wretched stream--

So, begone, O blessed flame,

Whilst I just sit and dream.

As The Fires Burn

HUMORESQUE IN RHYME

I'm se'mteen miles fum nowhare,
In a one-room cuntry shack--
De only thang I own on earth
Is haf whot's on my back.

De udder haf I "borrowed" fun Jim
When he wuz not about--
How cud I hitchhike outta heah
With haf o' me still out?

I s'pose ya wundin' how I cum
To be in sich a mess?
To tell the trufe, it's all my faut--
I mite as well confess.

Ya see, I had dis paht-time job
To wuik my way back eas'--
But den I made a mess duin'
A foath o' July feas'.

I thot de boss an' all hiz foaks
Had gone out fur de day--
So I'd jes fin' me su'um to swipe
To hep me on my way.

I made a surch thu-out de house
An' dare, under de stair,
I seed dis gret big ol' trunk
Mahked "Gold and silverware".

Now, git dis strate, I ain't no crook!
On honest, my foaks is big;
I jes needed a long-turm loan
Of sum li'l thang-a-majig.

I hurd de dawgs bahk 'cross de fiel',
But paid no 'tenchun to it.
I tuck a nife, unlocked de trunk,
An' started ramblin' thu it.

When I fus glanced inside I hurd
My conchus start to quibble--
But, man, de stuff inside dat trunk
Wud make a preechur dribble!

As The Fires Burn

64 - As The Fires Continue To Burn

I won't "Sam Jones" ya 'bout a thang,
Heah is de natual facks:
I went to reech inside dat trunk,
But friz rat in my tracks!

When I fus hurd dat pistol click,
An' hurd dat voice behind,
I didn't know whether to jes sit
Or haul off an' go blind.

De man done caught me fair an' square,
An' gid me sich a staht--
He thot to have me put away,
But had a change o' haht.

He sed, "Boy, ef I let you go,
Will de nex bus you be on?"
I sed, "Boss, jes let me go,
An' I'll ketch de one dat's gone!"

Den, sho a-nuff, he let me go
Wit jes a repurmand--
An', man, you shooda seen me split
Across dat fresh plowed land!

My Best To You

He changed hiz min' and shot two times
Jes as I jumped a wire--
Den I commenced to lo-mo run,
Lak a fox wid hiz tail on fire.

I don't know why he changed hiz min',
But glad hiz site wusn't true--
A li'l bit closer to my
hed, I wulda prob'ly jumped up an flew!

De way I plowed dem cohn fiel's up
It wuz a cryin' shame--
When ol' boss sees hiz crops digged up,
He got only hiz self to blame.

I moved on 'cross dat swamp so fas'
It seemed like runnin' on air--
I retch the shack and peeped aroun'
To see ef my shadow got dare.

I made it back to Jim's ol' place
Jes 'fore de sun went down--
I thot I'd sneak out be the gate
An' hitch my way to town.

As The Fires Burn

66 - As The Fires Continue To Burn

Still sem'teen miles fum nowhare,

Still in a one-room shack--

Ain't got no cloze to leave in now,

Ya see, Jim jes got back.

MAN IN THE MOON OVER DOUGLAS

Man up in the moon over Douglas,
Streaking Coffee skies with gold and blue--
Is it true about your beams,
Do they fashion lovers' dreams?
Do you make their dreams of happiness come true?

Man up in the moon over Douglas,
I once had a lover of my own.
We loved, we laughed, we cried,
Then love faded and died . . .
I just turned around and she was gone.

Man up in the moon over Douglas,
Will you cast a magic spell for me?
From your place up above,
Please help me find my love . . .
Shed your rays of love for her to see.

Dear old man of ages, I implore you,
Cast your magic through her window pane!
Speak to her as she sleeps,
Tell her my poor heart weeps;
Say I love her, and I want her back again.

As The Fires Burn

EYES ON THE SPARROW

Hello, li'l sparrow on the hill,
Is that a smile I see?
Is that your way
Of trying to say
You're not afraid of me?

Ah, so you take cookie from my hand,
And sip my lemonade . . .
So, there we see,
Trust is the key
To banning fear's charade.

Bravo, my little feathered friend!
Now I have news for you--
Your fount of love
Flowing from above
Is my sustenance, too.

As you are not afraid to stretch
Your wings and roam the skies,
Likewise am I
Undaunted by
Satan's sinistrous guise.

My Best To You

The Master of the universe,

Is at our beck and call--

With love sublime,

He'll take the time

To catch us if we fall.

So, chirp, chirp, my little friend,

Sing, hop, and make a fuss--

Let tree tops ring,

And nature sing:

"This world belongs to us."

70 - As The Fires Continue To Burn

ODE TO MY SISTER RUBY

It was not so long ago

God smiled upon us

and

He must have felt our loneliness

for He granted us the loan

a precious jewel

to

light up our life

I was much too young

to

remember the occasion

but

perhaps

because of her beauty and warmth

they called her

RUBY

My Best To You

Poetry By Carlo Crozatti - 71

A few nights ago

our loan period was up

and

God called

His precious jewel back to Himself

That night

I diligently searched the skies

for

in spite of the ominous cloud

I believe

a new star was born

I hope, trust, and believe

that

when they search for a name

among God's precious gems

because of her brilliance

her warmth

and her beauty

the angels will

call her

RUBY

As The Fires Burn

CHARLIE, GLADYS, AND ME

"Twas oh, so very long ago --
Although it doesn't seem quite so --
When we were kids out on the farm,
Causing their folks no small alarm;
But never meaning any harm...
Just Charlie, Gladys, and me.

The search for bird eggs in the straw,
The thrills up on the old seesaw;
The crawfish from our own coulees
Cooked in our house up in the trees
With pilfered honey from neighbor's bees...
Yep, Charlie, Gladys, and me.

The early morning trek for wood
Across the Barlow neighborhood...
The three of us with burlap sacks
Me, being the elder, with the axe,
The north wind thrashing at the backs...
Of Charlie, Gladys, and me.

Then came the sad and dreary day
When Uncle Sam called me away,
To enroll in a lethal game -
To visit places without name.
Life never would be quite the same
For Charlie, Gladys, and me.

I made it back across the sea,
But found noone to welcome me.
The grand home coming we had planned
Had been postponed by grim demand;
Charun had rowed across the land
Of Charlie, Gladys, and me.

Now they're gone, and I'm left here
To live in dreams of yesteryear --
But in the near, sweet by and by,
On that big farm up in the sky,
A three-point star'll appear on high...
Charlie, Gladys, and me.

As The Fires Burn

74 - As The Fires Continue To Burn

HOLD THE BABY

(Luke 2:25-32)

When Christ was born, long, long ago
And very far away,
A man of God named Simeon
Rejoiced to see His day.

Then took he Him up in his arms
And glorified the Lord,
"Now let your servant depart in peace,
According to your word.

"Mine eyes have seen your salvation,
(Which proves to all you cared),
The glory of the Israelites,
And all the world prepared."

So, friend, when life would get you down
And seems all hope is gone,
Just hold The Baby in your heart--
You'll never be alone.

My Best To You

Tho friends may turn their back on you
And tears your eyes may fill,
Lift up your head, beloved one,
And hold The Baby still.

Then, after time has disappeared,
Somewhere beyond the blue;
You'll feel the comfort of His arms,
For He will then hold you.

ODE TO A ROMAN TREE

High on a hill, somewhere in Rome,
A lonely tree yet stands
To guard a small but sacred spot
Where three lovers held hands.

"Oh no!" they say, "but three's a crowd,
It's two that's company!"
But you and I remember when
Sheer bliss was shared by three.

We stood beneath the Latin sky
And wished upon a star;
And though, how sad to find such love,
One must venture so far.

As she and I stood 'neath your limbs,
A zephyr touched your tips;
And as you shivered in the breeze,
A blossom kissed her lips.

'Twas then we knew that we'd be friends
Throughout all times to be,
To share a magic only found
In companies of three.

So when you hear some hapless soul
Lament that three's a crowd,
Remember her, remember me,
And say with head unbowed...

"Aha, my friend, if only you
Could share mem'ries with me . . .
A Roman night, a garden wall,
A girl, a boy, a tree.

78 - As The Fires Continue To Burn

WESTERN SKY WATCH

Day ends in anguish
Sol sheds excess energy
Earth glows with his flame.

Poetry By Carlo Crozatti

FAMILY AFFAIR

The boy was sent far off to school,
His balancing of budgets wasn't cool --
He spent all he had
Then wired to his dad:
"No mon, no fun. Your son."

The old man was still out on the farm
When he got his son's wire of alarm...
More cash he had none,
So he wired to his son:
"Too bad, too sad. Your dad."

As The Fires Burn

LAKE WATCH

Starfish deep breathing
Exercise unsuccessful
Toxins seined in gill.

WEATHER FORECAST

Mares' tails daubs the sky

Sky gods give thund'rous praise to

Bad weather ahead.

82 - As The Fires Continue To Burn

IF I FAILED TO LOVE YOU

(Ma Ti Voglia Bene)

If I failed to love you,
Songs of the popinjay
Would slowly fade away --
Rivers would no longer claim the sea.
There'd be no time for things
Like wedding bells and rings --
The whippoorwill would lose his melody.

If I failed to love you,
There'd be no harvest moon,
No flowers grown in June;
Merchants would discard their silk and lace.
No Gypsy's violin
His love song would begin . . .
The man up in the moon would hide his face.

Skies would ne'er be clear,
No rainbows would appear --
Spring rains would refuse to leave the sky.
Ergo, no rolling hills
Covered with daffodils . . .
The oceans' roar would dwindle to a sigh.

My Best To You

If I failed to love you,
Euterpe's charms would fade
Into a masquerade,
The Mona Lisa's smile would be a frown.
The soothing summer breeze
Would not caress the trees . . .
The ancient pyramids would tumble down.

If I failed to love you,
Summer would come in fall,
There'd be no spring at all;
All flowers would just simply fade away.
No drops of honeydew,
Roses, or violets blue . . .
No withered memories of yesterday.

If I failed to love you,
Orion would protest,
The North Star would go west;
The Milky Way would show its temperament.
The sun would glower by day,
The moon would phase away . . .
All heaven would display its discontent.

As The Fires Burn

84 - As The Fires Continue To Burn

If I failed to love you,

Angels up above

Would nullify my love;

No mortal being my wretched heart could touch

So think as I confess

To you with tenderness,

"Ti voglia bene!," I love you very much.

MERRY CHRISTMAS, LTD.

I remember the phrase, "Merry Christmas!"
I remember the joy it used to bring --
The thrill of bobsleds coasting,
The smell of chestnuts roasting;
The many happy songs we loved to sing.

I remember the fires burning brightly,
The snowflakes like stardust in your hair --
The looks we used to get
When they knew our lips had met;
The way you smiled and whispered, "I don't care."

I remember the socks hung by the fire,
The notes we wrote that never were quite true.
The flickering lamp light,
Our final kiss good night--
The lonely walk that led away from you.

I remember our strolls in the moonlight,
But, to you, it all was just a game.
You never said good-bye,
Just "domani," with a sigh;
But, alas, tomorrow never came.

As The Fires Burn

86 - As The Fires Continue To Burn

I remember the phrase, "Merry Christmas!"

But only with memories of pain.

If somehow Santa's charms

Could return you to my arms,

Then Christmas would be merry once again.

GUEST POETS SECTION

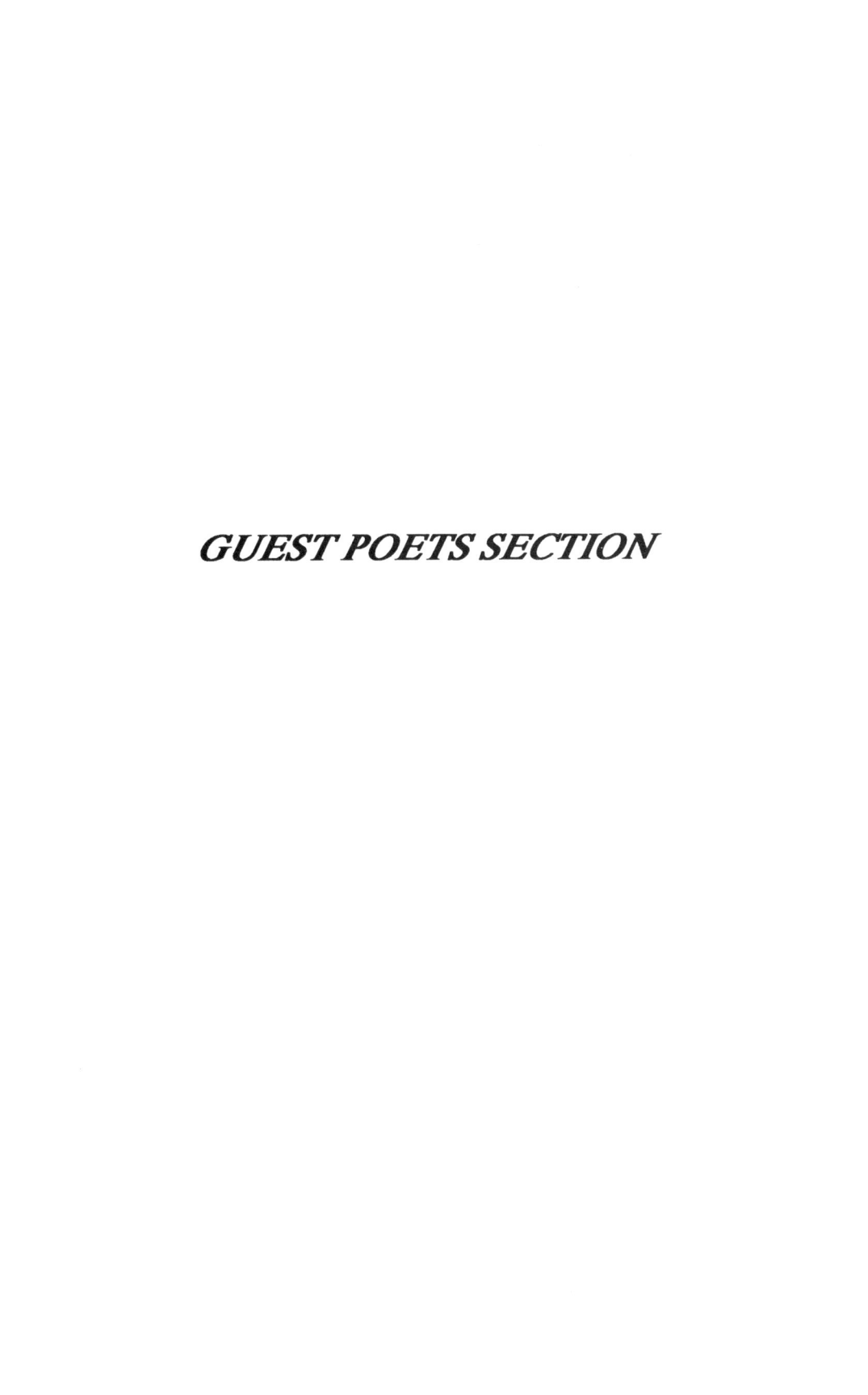

Guest Index

90. Kandi Brigmond - I Am The Sun

92. David Busby - Dreams

93. Latoya Butler - This Little Flower

94. Melissa Butler - Longing, But Afraid

96. Selena Butler - The Shore

98. John Crawford - My Window Of The World

100. Kimberley Cubbage - He Used To...

101. Kurt Deen - Storm On The Horizon

103. Nick G. Donkar - Why Classify?

104. Teena Foca - Gymnast

106. Tracy Graham - Pollution

107. Anthony Hardy - The Watcher

109. Tareem Heath - There Is A Place For Me

112. Dena Hutchins - A Heart's Desire

113. Andrew Jenklin - I Stand Alone

114. Robert Jordan - What Is A Black Man?

Guest Index

(Continued)

115. Jeff Larkey - A Single, Shadowed Wanderer

117. Laquinta Lewis - The Search Within

119. Tracie Lewis - The Sad Sunset

120. Dennis Narh-Martey - When The Oak Sends Its Roots Abroad

122. Salita McClelland - You And Me

124. Collin B. McQueen - Night Of Passion

125. Wendy Morris - Digging

126. Melvin Pace - Life

127. April Pellock - I Tremble

129. Masayu Ramli - What Is Love

131. Steven Richard Robinson - Parody For The Children Of The Wind

133. Mack Smart - My Faith In God

134. Michele White - My Heart Only Aches

135. Wesley K. Wilson - Hate Is Home

90 - As The Fires Continue To Burn

I AM THE SUN

AND YOU ARE MY RAYS

I am the sun
And you are my rays...
Without you, love,
I would have no ways.

I am just plain,
But when you come my way
You bring something extra
To help on my way.

You came along --
I was aching inside..
But somehow, or another,
I shoved it aside.

You made my happy,
You made me gay...
When I was downhearted,
You brightened my day.

My Best To You

Now you've become
A great part of me --
How could I've dreamed
Of such ecstasy?

Whether or not
My mien chose to show
My life is your life --
I want you should know.

I am the sun
And you are my rays...
Without you, love,
I would have no ways.

Kandi Brigmond
Douglas, Georgia

DREAMS

Dreams are stories told deep in the night
Hidden secrets in the back of your mind
A mixture of thought, emotion, and fear
Across a subconscious stage will appear

Are there questions to answer
Unasked by the voice
Dealt with each night
Often without choice

Fleeting impressions of your day shoot past
Heart beats quicken from slow to fast
Cobwebs of sleep are chased by dawn
Memory lapses after a yawn

David Busby
Nicholls, Georgia

THIS LITTLE FLOWER

This little flower
Big and bright;
This little flower
Shines at night.

This little flower
Stands out like a star,
And people notice it
Where ever they are.

This little flower's
Name is kindness,
A quality given only
To the finest.

Latoya Butler
Broxton, Georgia

LONGING, BUT AFRAID

Trusting who we believe in,

Afraid to get close, but giving easy like a sin.

Eager when it's time to call,

Afraid they're not going to be around the next time I fall.

Reaching out with soul and heart,

Afraid of their leaving or growing apart.

Telling the mind you can learn a lot --

Afraid of another piece breaking off in that slot.

Searching for every moment in the life...

Afraid of the good-byes which cut like a knife.

Dealing every day with anger and fear,

Afraid to let them know when I shed a tear.

Finally feeling I can do things that other people dare --

Afraid to hate them when I really do care.

Poetry By Carlo Crozatti - 95

Bringing out colors in the fire,

Afraid of the future of what I desire.

Wishing no one was there to help and to hold...

Afraid of advice that has been thought through and told.

Thinking too much in my mind,

Afraid of letting the walls down for what I might find.

Only taking chances that I've already done,

Afraid of the new disappointments that come one after one.

Melissa Butler
Broxton, Georgia

As The Fires Burn

THE SHORE

Cool breeze upon my face,
The water rushes in...
Beautiful little flowers
Washed up on the sand.

Creatures wearing armor
As if crawling off the war --
Fighting for their survival
On the sandy shore.

Water beats the rocks
With anger, fury, and rage...
Down upon the horizon,
The old light shows its age.

Then the night crawls in,
Watching for the new day...
The faded one being over-
Old and gone away.

My Best To You

Soon the light will peek
Over the tall dancing grass...
And another beautiful day
Starts just like the last.

Selena Butler
Ambrose, Georgia

MY WINDOW OF THE WORLD

I look through the window out on the world,
    At the atrocities committed daily,
    At those who just sit there and watch it happen,
    And I pity them as I pity those who have felt
    The full face of the world at its cruelest.
    Forgotten with each new day,
    Replaced as there are more to remember.
    Remembered only by those few who were close,
    And even they have a hard time remembering.
    And with the passage of those who would remember,
    More will be forgotten.

What can be done?
    Nothing if you are weak.
    War and violence will not stop,
    While there are those who are willing to fight,
    Nor will it stop if those who do not fight,
    Will not fight,
    To stop the fighting.
    To be virtuous is good,

But your virtue will not stop the viciousness.

The task will overwhelm you if you let it;

DON'T.

John Crawford
Douglas, Georgia

100 - As The Fires Continue To Burn

HE USED TO . . .

He used to be a vibrant man,

He used to play with my brother in the sand,

He used to take us to play in the park,

Talk to us for hours when it was dark,

He used to cook and he used to clean,

When he was sober he was never mean,

He used to drink,

He used to drive,

42 years later my daddy died,

Now he can't do the things he used to,

Because of drinking his life is through.

Now there is something I must request of you,

If my dad were here he would to;

Please don't let drinking do this to you.

Dedicated to the memory of
Mr. David Lee Cubbage
Kimberley Cubbage
Savannah, Georgia

My Best To You

STORM ON THE HORIZON

The storm had just gathered a mighty shield
To block the desert heat.
The land was quiet and peaceful,
until the clouds did meet.

They hung in the sky for months,
and made the day as night.
Then, all of a sudden, the floodgates opened,
and the storm let loose its might.

It raged on for days and days,
and nowhere was there calm.
The clouds moved with the speed of jets,
and the lightning exploded like bombs.

And then the storm was over and done,
the desert replenished, but scarred.
And though the land was burning,
one thing had not been marred.

As The Fires Burn

102 - As The Fires Continue To Burn

The courage and strength of the people

has lasted and stayed true.

And in the sky was a rainbow,

colored red, white, and blue.

Kurt Deen
Broxton, Georgia

WHY CLASSIFY?

White

Black

Hispanic

Asian

Oriental

Other

Everyone is asked to circle one

Can someone explain why this is done?

To classify an individual is to limit

Why should we have to be placed in it?

People are people, so why should it be?

To classify each one of us prohibits racial harmony

Nick G. Donkar
Savannah, Georgia

GYMNAST

Patience is man's greatest virtue,
Or so the saying goes;
A gymnast must have said it,
For a gymnast surely knows.

That in this funny sport of ours
Discouragement runs high,
And, at times, the best will find
That patience passed us by.

When hands are ripped and throbbing,
When every muscle's sore --
Can a gymnast still have patience
To limp in for some more?

When you've lost old moves You used to do,
And progress seems so slow,
Can you still have faith in better days
And not feel sad and low?

Can you admit you're frightened
Yet not give into fears?
Can you defeat frustration and
Conquer pain and tears?

When someone else does something
You've tried so long to do,
Can you really feel glad for him
Or just feel pity for you?

And when success seems far away,
Your efforts all in vain,
Can you force yourself to wear a smile
And disregard the pain?

If, despite the tribulations,
You never once give in,
You will see that winners
Do not always win.

Teena Foca
Savannah, Georgia

106 - As The Fires Continue To Burn

POLLUTION

The air is getting thick, it's hard to breathe.
Away went the animals and plants we so badly need.

The rivers and waters are foggy with trash.
Our fish are all dying, the rate pretty fast.

Pollution from everywhere is destroying our air.
We all must clean it, we all need to care.

No one seems to think about the future,
Or our children's pain and torture.

One day our planet will no longer be.
It's all our fault, we're full of greed.

Tracy Graham
Savannah, Georgia

My Best To You

THE WATCHER

She rides,

lonely,

Only she and her steed,

No other Souls;

None...

the nearest is

forever far.

Her hair-

silky darkness-

Flows gracefully

As she and her mount of white

Transverse the plain of gloom.

Her eyes,

diamonds of black,

Scintillate in the silvery moonlight.

As The Fires Burn

108 - As The Fires Continue To Burn

Her skin,

As a pearl in the night.

Mountains of Blue

crested with white,

rise solemnly behind Her,

as she passes...

silently...

never knowing **that** one,

one who loves her so dearly,

Is so near;

Yet so far...

Forever Far.

Anthony Hardy
Douglas, Georgia

My Best To You

THERE IS A PLACE FOR ME

There is a special place in life,

That needs my humble skill,

A certain job I'm meant to do,

Nobody else can fill.

The hours are demanding,

And the pay is not too good,

And yet, I wouldn't change it

For a moment, if I could.

There is a special place in life,

A goal I must attain,

A dream that I must follow,

For I won't be back again,

As The Fires Burn

110 - As The Fires Continue To Burn

There is a mark that I must leave,

However small it be,

A legacy of love for those

Who follow after me.

There is a special place in life,

That only I may share.

A little path that bears my name,

Awaiting me somewhere.

There is a hand that I must hold,

A word that I must say,

A smile that I must give,

For there are tears to blot away.

There is a special place in life,

That I was meant to fill,

A sunny spot where flowers grow

Upon a windy hill.

My Best To You

There's always a tomorrow.

And the best is yet to be,

And somewhere in this world I know

There is a place for me!

Tareem Heath
Savannah, Georgia

A HEART'S DESIRE

He looks at his competition with weary eyes,

The desire burns inside like a hot burning fire.

He has waited for this moment for years

The ever consuming dream he has is finally coming true

A sharp noise causes a stir in his system

Suddenly the gun sounds, the race begun

All he hears and all he thinks is how much he wants this

He does not care that his competitors are faster

He does not care that right now they are ahead of him

Dramatically quick he darts out ahead of the others

He pushes himself with all of his might

He comes to the end and the ribbon falls

He has won the race

His heart's desire has given him his dream.

Dena Hutchins
Douglas, Georgia

I STAND ALONE

I stand alone
    In a room filled with a hundred people
    I talk, laugh, smile with them all
    But inside -
    I stand alone
    In a room filled with a hundred people.

Andrew Jenklin
Savannah, Georgia

114 - As The Fires Continue To Burn

WHAT IS A BLACK MAN

Proud is he who

Rates himself highly.

Strong is he who

Works hard and is brave.

Dignified is he who

Is self-worthy and challenging.

Ambitious is he who

Is eager for power.

Diligent worker is he who

Gets the job done.

Self supportive is he who,

Chooses to take control.

Leader is he who

conquers The soul

These are what qualify a black man.

Robert Jordan
Savannah, Georgia

My Best To You

A SINGLE, SHADOWED WANDERER

A single, shadowed wanderer
Stood upon the forlorn shore,
Looking ahead towards an enlightenment
Forever beyond his desperate grasp.
Standing as stone in the briny epitaph
Framed by luminescence born
In a past beyond remembrance.

About his feet lay a rotted weave
And in his hand
The rusted sextant
Primeval symbols of explorers long dead.

Beneath his salt speckled brow
Somber eyes gleamed
Reflecting the eternal grave of the sea.
The sorrow for lost mysteries
Flowed from those eyes...
Tracing corridors through
Time wrought canyons,
And if he shifted at all

As The Fires Burn

116 - As The Fires Continue To Burn

It remained unseen.

The mountains of the moon

Forever guard their secrets

And grey seems to elude

The most piercing gaze

Jeff Larkey
Douglas, Georgia

THE SEARCH WITHIN

Am I really here?
Do I paint a road that is not yet paved?
Do I look at life's most incessant days?
Do I look at the hills from which I came?
Am I really here?

The thought about reality is a glass bottle,
Thinking that all you dream for is impossible.
Maybe this is true, maybe this is true--
Maybe you fell into a deep hole that
Surrounded your thoughts,
Thinking, never knowing, that
there was something to set apart.

Am I dreaming...
Am I living in my dark shadow?
Am I a dream or an illusion?
My mind is filled with extreme confusion.

The Supreme Being is closely related to your heart.

As The Fires Burn

118 - As The Fires Continue To Burn

Standing there with open arms,

But where does the pain ever stop?

Does it look in my face every time I fall asleep?

Every time I close my eyes, my mind never sees relief.

The pain gets stronger and then I'm off far away. Finding myself in a battle --

A battle to see who is going to win.

Do I have the victory over everything?

The thoughts of it make it known I'll never gain.

Never thought that it would be true,

You will find happiness in this world, Yes you...

My thoughts of you never seem to touch.

Love is only an object I feel and that's not so much.

The only things I can rest upon are things above.

I will say to myself, "I need you LOVE,

I NEED YOU LOVE!"

Laquinta Lewis
Savannah, Georgia

THE SAD SUNSET

As I sit I converse with the sunset

It looks as if the sunset is sad

It calls out saying "I wish I could continue to shine"

I say to him "Your time will come again

and you shall shine brightly on the earth"

The sun continues to fade

The colors of orange and red become deeper and deeper

The night falls

A very deep darkness covers the earth

I realize instantaneously that my conversation was over

I fall asleep

I arise to notice a very lively and bright shining sun

I say "I told you that you would shine again"

Tracie Lewis
Savannah, Georgia

120 - As The Fires Continue To Burn

DEATH; WHEN THE OAK SENDS ITS ROOTS ABROAD

Death, death, death...

Death is common,

But we know not when, where, or how it happens.

Humans born, Humans die.

The star falls, the death calls,

The curlew calls

And darkness settles on roofs.

Yes, yes, morning goes, evening comes,

When my tongue utters the thoughts that arise in me;

That's when man dies.

At the bottom of my feet, that's where I keep

The list of the dead people.

But the worst part is

Whosoever is dead will never come back.

My Best To You

Poetry By Guest Poets - 121

When man sleeps I work;

That's why dead bodies look like sleeping bodies.

I kill any time I choose,

But yet there is no power who cares

Mr. Grave is my chief advisor

And always tells me,

"Death, immediately you kill!

I am ready to put it under ground."

Yes, that's how I am.

To my destruction, spoiled,

made base by vainer things.

Damned sins to you, but not to me

because I have the license to kill.

This fray seems not only to you

but to all mankind.

When the oak sends his roots abroad,

That's when I let man's spirit think

they are in a resting place.

Dennis Marh-Martey
Savannah, Georgia

As The Fires Burn

YOU AND ME

Together we have laughed and had great moments
And shared happiness and dreams;
We've talked through our differences and misunderstandings
And found what true love really means.

We confide in each other with the darkest of secrets
That the normal couple couldn't endure with help from above;
Together, we can overcome anything that stands in our way
With our special and unique thing called love.

I can reach out to you and you to me
Although our hands are so far apart;
You can say and do special things without being near me
That touch my lonely, empty heart.

If there was only one drop of water on earth
With you I would gladly share that one sip;
Because, together we have taught each other something new
That's blended with a lifetime of pure friendship.

If I were the poorest of the poor, or the weakest of the weak
With only you I would feel rich and strong;
If ever that gloomy day comes and we foolishly fall apart
There would always be a place in me you'd belong.

Whenever we have arguments like normal couples do
Think of how much I love you and need you so;
Think of how far we've come together as one
Although we still have a long road to go.

Think of how special and meaningful our lives could be.
Think of it always, constantly,
because it is two special people . . .
"You and Me"

Salita McClelland
Douglas, Georgia

124 - As The Fires Continue To Burn

NIGHT OF PASSION

The moon sits in the sky like a beautiful white pearl.
Wind blows gently through our hair.
Lying on the sandy beach,
She looks into my eyes with much love and compassion.
The waves are beating up against each other.
Her face is like a red rose that blossomed during the summer.
She's delicate, innocent, but very fragile,
And with the voice of angel
And such beauty that has never been captured.
She takes her delicate hand
And grabs my big huge chest tightly.
Rolling in the sand, flying in air,
And swimming in the sea of love and passion.
Never to die,
Our hearts standing at the gates of love and freedom,
Never to be separated,
In joy, love, and peace forever.

Collin B. McQueen
Douglas, Georgia

My Best To You

DIGGING

I am enclosed,

Just enough to breathe.

I begin to scratch and claw,

Falling away are scraps and remnants of theories

experimental solutions.

I tug heartily at my family,

It falls past my feet.

I shovel a layer of standards, rules, and society,

They constantly compile, you know, I must move faster.

Move harder...

I must move,

For a pressuring eternity is looming, constantly surrounding.

For one day I know I will reach a final barrier,

It's glass, you know.

Luminescence is pending...

Not the strongest weapon in the world can break it.

Whether or not the final barrier is shattered ...

is up to me.

Wendy Morris
Savannah, Georgia

As The Fires Burn

126 - As The Fires Continue To Burn

LIFE

What is life?
To some a gift, a pain, a bore.
But in my view, life is like the most precious gift,
Greater than gold or any riches.

Some people are taking life for granted.
Then on the other hand, some take their life and master it.
The birds, the trees, fresh air, are abundant
And all a part of life.

I often remember the times when I was younger,
Wishing I knew then what I know now.
But we get elder, we get wiser,
And I found that out for a fact.

I promise myself to endure my life
And conquer goals impossible to some,
To live my life fully
Every day.

Melvin Pace
Douglas, Georgia

My Best To You

I TREMBLE

I tremble,

And glass shatters.

Once more-

A sound

And a chill that warms me. It tingles.

I reach out for more,

But it is too far.

More shattering,

And a blackness that burns me-

Scorching my soul.

An aching fills me,

But I can no longer escape it.

The bowl stares at me

As the contents of my companion churn elsewhere.

I stare back,

Leaving the sage words of my elders behind

To haunt those who choose the same path I chose.

Water flows,

As The Fires Burn

128 - As The Fires Continue To Burn

And I suffer.

I retreat to the burning blackness

Of my stubborn ways,

Failing myself forever.

April Pellock
Savannah, Georgia

WHAT IS LOVE?

Love is whispering sweet things

into his ears.

Love is listening to him scream

'till he brings you into tears

Love is kissing under the stars

in the moonlight.

Love is being cursed at

during a terrible fight.

Love is telling him

secrets you have never told before.

Love is watching him yawn;

a sign that you're a bore,

Love is getting along great

with one another.

Love is being worst enemies

As The Fires Burn

130 - As The Fires Continue To Burn

with his mother.

Love is saying

"I love you"

Love is hearing

"I'm sorry, I cheated on you. ~

Love is being together

for a long time.

Love is breaking up; it's bitter

and sourer than lime.

Isn't it great being in love?

You feel like you're on top of the clouds above.

But be careful - it's a long, long fall....

One slip, and it will be the end of it all!

Masayu Ramli
Savannah, Georgia

A PARODY FOR THE CHILDREN OF THE WIND

Sing, painted maiden!
Sing of the lands that were once held sacred--
the land that was your birthright--
the land that, through the eons,
your people have come to revere,
that supplied your heart-shine.
For long gone are the days
when elk, water buffalo, bison and wilderbeest
provided challenge for your brave warriors --
when he hunted with respect
beside coyote, hyena, brothers,
brothers of the windsong.

Sing, painted maiden!
The tribal princes and princesses
no longer hold sacred
the traditions and rituals
of husbandry and the healing arts,
spirit gifts from nature.

As The Fires Burn

132 - As The Fires Continue To Burn

Sing, painted maiden!

Sing quietly, sing softly,

for little papoose, Ndoyo Lala

has been frightened by the night sounds.

Could it be the far off sounds of the ancestors

extolling tales of glorious bygone heroes?

(Hiawatha, Dshango of Ojibwa,

Mwindo of the brave Apache;

Zulu and Arapahoe-Mali people)

long before the day of the white man . . .

Sing, painted maiden!
Sing with tears of reverence,
for tears of grief and regret
are not welcome here.
The winds of change have swept the land--
you must teach a song of rebirth;
you must learn a song of worlds beyond you . . .

This, painted maiden,
is the song you must mold
into the little one's awareness;
for they are the ones
who are to inherit
the wind.

Steven Richard Robinson
Chicago, Illinois

My Best To You

MY FAITH IN GOD

I pray to the Lord each and every day
To guide my mind and light my way
When I lay my head down to sleep
I put my faith in my hands and pray
I often wonder will I make it through the day
He watches over me always
Even when I'm not really there.
The young and the old seem to pass me by
I've always been told to keep my head towards the sky
It gets real hard sometimes but I still must try
And I keep my Faith in God.
This world does not care about what I want or do
But someone above is watching
Someone who believes in me
And I believe in Him just as much
Yes, I must keep my Faith in God.

Mack Smart
Savannah, Georgia

MY HEART ONLY ACHES

Golden brown hair that falls gently
Over your soft hazel eyes,
The eyes that are staring so strongly into mine.
So tall with beauty's firm structure and grace,
I reach out to touch your loving such face.
I attempt to put my arms around you, to hold you tight,
But it is all a fantasy on this cold, lonely night.

Don't leave me now when I need you the most,
Give me a chance to be with you and not your ghost.
You are only an image in the corners of my mind,
That I can lose at any unknown time.

Why can't you understand I need you with me,
that is the only way that I can be free.

Amy Michele White
Savannah, Georgia

HATE IS HOME

Hated by the good of heart,
Respected by the darkest souls --
Men dwell in hate, refusing to show
Sensitivity for their tolls.

Unacknowledged is hate's existence
For the preference of love...
There is none without the other,
And no other is above.

Love, the adversary of hate,
The enemy of sin and wrong...
The opposition of despise-
Love's weak while hate is strong!

Hatred is a strong defense;
No one can wander in...
For hate controls the only key
To hell's eternal sin.

As The Fires Burn

136 - As The Fires Continue To Burn

Hate is strength...

Hate is protection...

HATE IS HOME!

Wesley K. Wilson
Savannah, Georgia

My Best To You